Arranged for Easy Piano
by Dan Coates

Music From

STAR WARS®

EPISODE I
THE PHANTOM MENACE™

By JOHN WILLIAMS

Project Manager: CAROL CUELLAR
Book Art Layout: CARMEN FORTUNATO
Photography: WILLIAM CLAXTON

WARNER BROS. PUBLICATIONS - THE GLOBAL LEADER IN PRINT
USA: 15800 NW 48th Avenue, Miami, FL 33014

WARNER/CHAPPELL MUSIC

CANADA: 40 SHEPPARD AVE. WEST, SUITE 800
TORONTO, ONTARIO, M2N 6K9
SCANDINAVIA: P.O. BOX 533, VENDEVAGEN 85 B
S-182 15, DANDERYD, SWEDEN
AUSTRALIA: P.O. BOX 353
3 TALAVERA ROAD, NORTH RYDE N.S.W. 2113

Carisch
NUOVA CARISCH

ITALY: VIA CAMPANIA, 12
20098 S. GIULIANO MILANESE (MI)
ZONA INDUSTRIALE SESTO ULTERIANO
SPAIN: MAGALLANES, 25
28015 MADRID
FRANCE: 20, RUE DE LA VILLE-L'EVEQUE, 75008 PARIS

IMP
INTERNATIONAL MUSIC PUBLICATIONS LIMITED

ENGLAND: GRIFFIN HOUSE,
161 HAMMERSMITH ROAD, LONDON W6 8BS
GERMANY: MARSTALLSTR. 8, D-80539 MUNCHEN
DENMARK: DANMUSIK, VOGNMAGERGADE 7
DK 1120 KOBENHAVNK

CONTENTS

DUEL OF THE FATES

By JOHN WILLIAMS
Arranged by DAN COATES

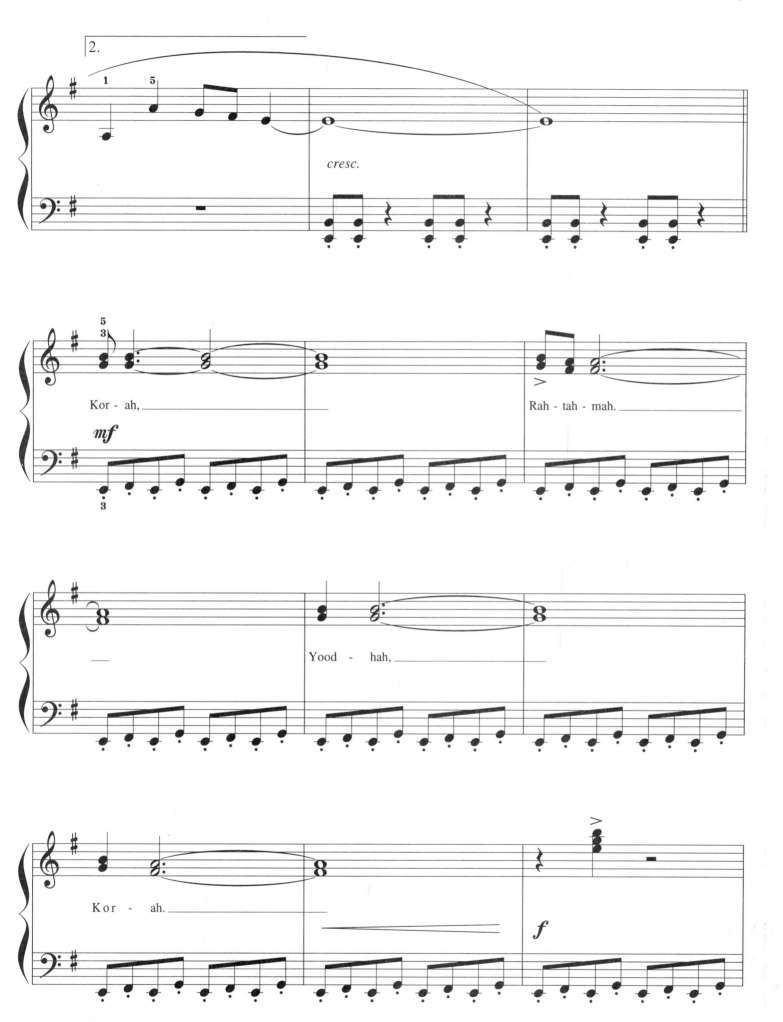

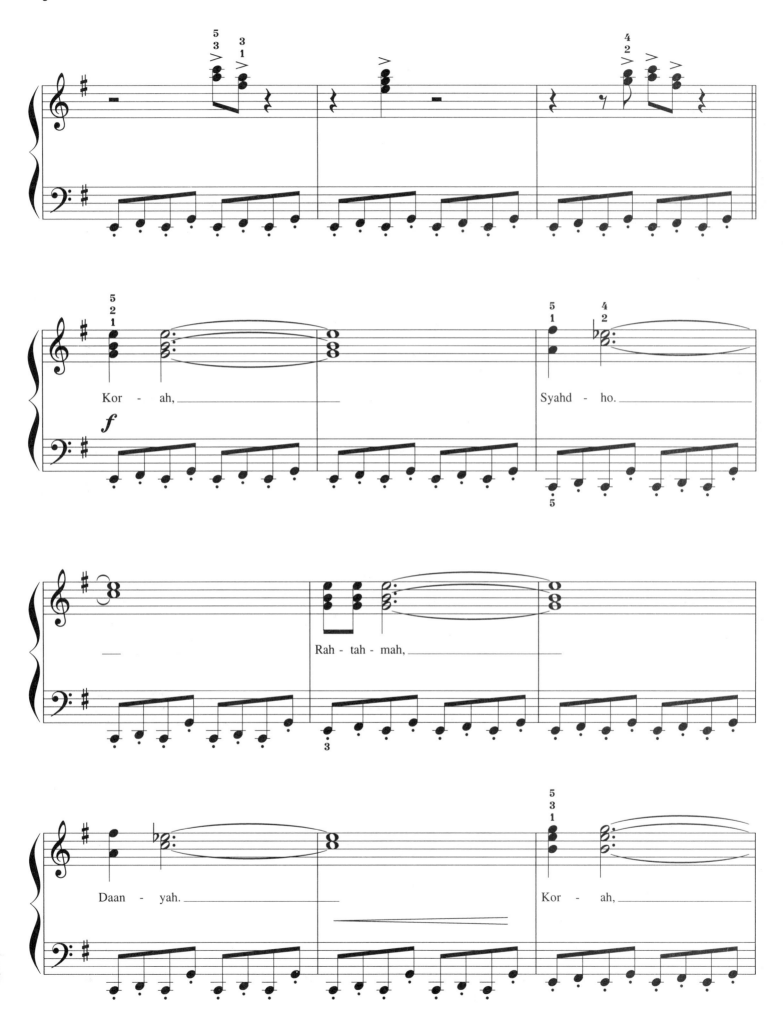

ANAKIN'S THEME

By JOHN WILLIAMS
Arranged by DAN COATES

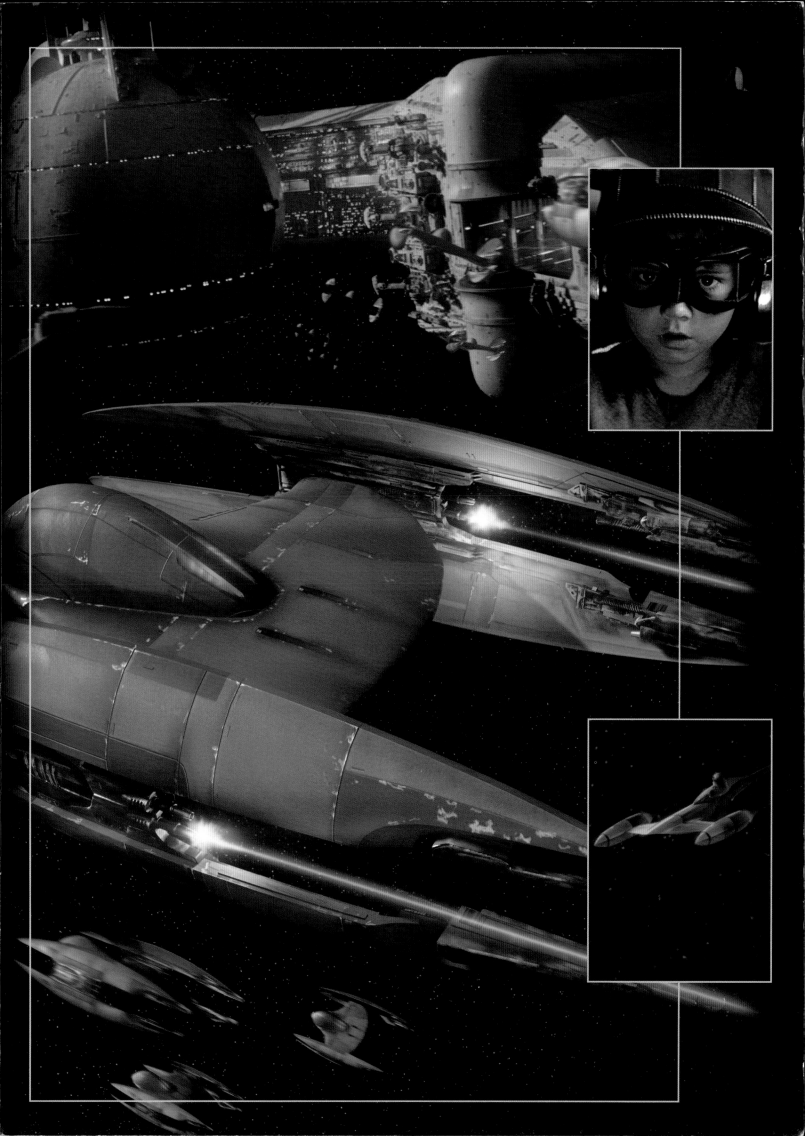

AUGIE'S GREAT MUNICIPAL BAND

By JOHN WILLIAMS
Arranged by DAN COATES

Joyously ♩ = 126

Augie's Great Municipal Band - 3 - 1

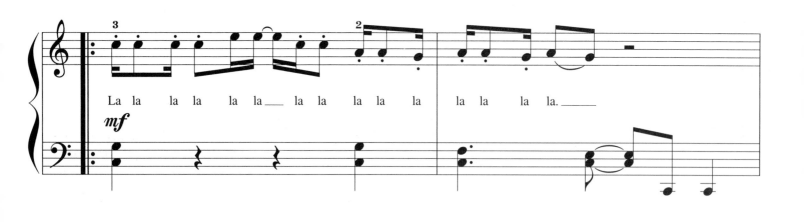

La la la la la la la la la la la la la la la.

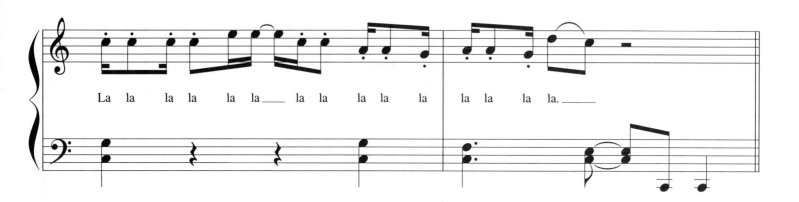

La la la la la la la la la la la la la la.

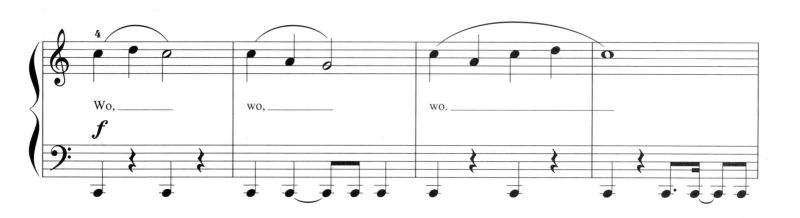

Wo, wo, wo.

Yah yah yah yah yah yah yah yah yah yah

JAR JAR'S INTRODUCTION

By JOHN WILLIAMS
Arranged by DAN COATES

QUI-GON'S FUNERAL

By JOHN WILLIAMS
Arranged by DAN COATES

Dirge, solemnly ♩ = 60

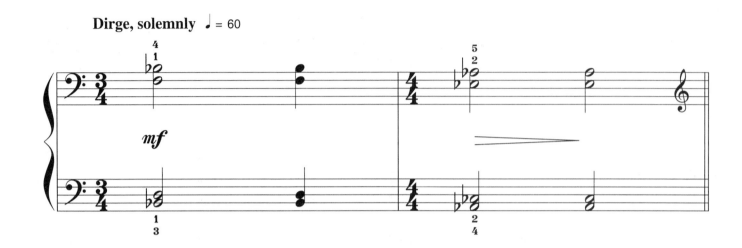

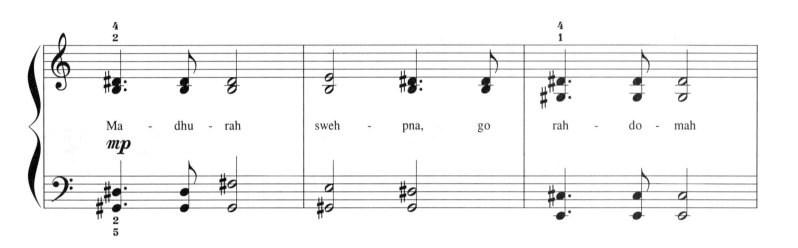

Ma - dhu - rah   sweh - pna,   go   rah - do - mah

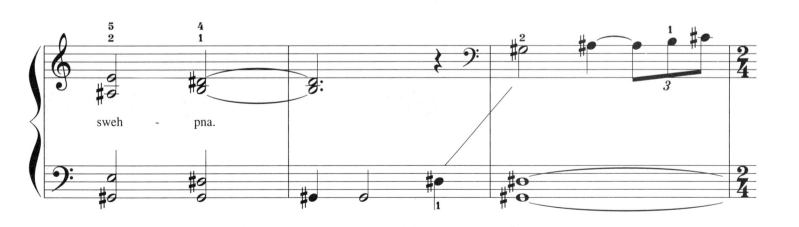

sweh - pna.

Qui-Gon's Funeral - 2 - 1

THE FLAG PARADE

By JOHN WILLIAMS
Arranged by DAN COATES

The Flag Parade - 4 - 1

STAR WARS
(Main Theme)

By JOHN WILLIAMS
Arranged by DAN COATES

Dan Coates

Photo: by Carin A. Baer

One of today's foremost personalities in the field of printed music, Dan Coates has been providing teachers and professional musicians with quality piano material since 1975. Equally adept in arranging for beginners or accomplished musicians, his Big Note, Easy Piano and Professional Touch arrangements have made a significant contribution to the industry.

Born in Syracuse, New York, Dan began to play piano at the age of four. By the time he was 15, he'd won a New York State competition for music composers. After high school graduation, he toured the United States, Canada and Europe as an arranger and pianist with the world-famous group Up With People.

Dan settled in Miami, Florida, where he studied piano with Ivan Davis at the University of Miami while playing professionally throughout southern Florida. To date, his performance credits include appearances on "Murphy Brown" and "My Sister Sam" and at the Opening Ceremonies of the 1984 Summer Olympics in Los Angeles. Dan has also accompanied such artists as Dusty Springfield and Charlotte Rae.

In 1982, Dan began his association with Warner Bros. Publications—an association that has produced more than four hundred Dan Coates books and sheets. Throughout the year, he conducts piano workshops nationwide, during which he demonstrates his popular arrangements.